Praise for *matwân cî*

I close the cover of Nia To Go There's new book, *matwân cî*, and lean back in my chair—calm, feeling an intense oneness with the earth, both simple and complex, filled with wonder. To Go There has laid out for us in her poems and the illustrative art that accompanies them, the journey of a people, and within that story the journey which is herself. Here is a book that travels through your bloodstream into your soul and heart. This poet holds the stories, the language, the dances, and visions of the sacred animals. She stands between worlds. The healing involves all of us and needs our awareness, our differences, our likeness to weave together what has been separated in and among all of us.

— Christin Lore Weber, author of *No This But This.*

Nia To Go There's new collection of poems often requires a good amount of sitting with. As a wild tangling and untangling of contemporary cultural worldviews (and their horrors) with traditional lifeways and experiences, To Go There's Poems illuminate, challenge, inspire and educate. Rich with imagery and at times deeply personal, the poems collected here flourish with multiple readings. So, I urge you, reader, to not put *matwân cî* on a timer. Allow the poems every moment they deserve, every moment they require of you. You will be better for the conversation.

— Chris La Tray, Montana Poet Laureate 2023-2025,
Little Shell Tribe of Chippewa Indians

Nia To Go There has provided a literary medley of mystical and wonderful poetry and poetic prose in her book, *matwân cî*. Her poems and prose are provocative and evocative in addressing the existential questions of identity, purpose, and direction through Indigenous thought and voice. Thank you for this gift of moving and inspirational poetry.

— Paul Hill, Jr., Founder,
National Rites of Passage Institute

matwân cî is a philosopher's wanderings, and wonderment about life itself. Nia To Go There harvests from her heart, a blossoming of spirit, a sojourner's quest for answers but like Einstein observes "a problem cannot be solved with the same consciousness that creates the problem." Sometimes "I just know" is what the poet knows. And she knows "I am not an observer, but a participant fundamentally entangled with the universe" and "human beings are not separate from nature but are nature." Storytelling, alive with thoughtfulness and humor enlightens and guides us to ponder, to question, and to be grateful for the intimacy and wonder of human connections and "why [we are] here.

— Sherry Quan Lee, Editor, *How Dare We! Write: A Multicultural Creative Writing Discourse*

matwân cî offers a window into a wide range of topics. Some of the poems are specific to Nia To Go There's experiences of being an Indigenous woman. Others are universal: for example, her keen and appreciative observations of the natural world. Readers will explore many new horizons in the care of a kind and wise guide. They are in good hands.

— Patricia Park
(One of Nia To Go There's former—and forever—students.)

Nia's poetry and poetic prose in *matwân cî* is a refreshing sigh of an authentically true and connected being. An honest experience is held in Nia's beautiful word images that sustain the paradoxes embodied and linked in all energies.

— Steph Hecker, LCSW, RPT

In the insanities of our world today, *matwân cî* reminds us to take a moment to be still… to experience deeply, profoundly a journey into the language of the unknown, yet known. A reminder of who we are. An invitation to become fully self, loving other. An honoring of the most beloved, Earth. Hers is a voice raised to reveal the lies we worship and a voice that inspires us to the truths of living wise and well.

— Wanda Daniel, Earth Minister

We are both visible and invisible. We are sacred and must open ourselves to our own story…waiting to be told." With these words Nia To Go There invites us to accompany her on a journey into an ancient space that transcends time, to a place in which first peoples live within the sacred sphere of the earth. She is re-minding us in *matwân cî* of the language and practices of her ancestors. To Go There offers a way to bring these languages and practices into our own stories, which wait to weave us into the fabric of the living cosmos. Spoken in many different voices of native people, these poems and reflections, simply, offer profound love to the world.

— Kathleen Jesme, author of
The Loneliness of a Planet Without a Moon

Modern History Press

Ann Arbor, MI

IBSN 979-8-89656-038-8 paperback
IBSN 979-8-89656-039-5 hardcover
IBSN 979-8-89656-040-1 eBook

Published by
Modern History Press   ModernHistoryPress.com
5145 Pontiac Trail   info@ModernHistoryPress.com
Ann Arbor, MI 48105

Distributed by Ingram Content Group (USA, CAN, EU, UK, AU)

Library of Congress Cataloging-in-Publication Data
Names: To Go There, Nia, author. | Rittenhouse, Stephanie, illustrator.
Title: Matwân cî : …wondering about now and then and everything everywhere / Nia To Go There ; illustrated by Stephanie Rittenhouse.
Description: Ann Arbor, MI : Modern History Press, [2025] | Includes bibliographical references. | Summary: "As a wild tangling and untangling of contemporary cultural worldviews (and their horrors) with traditional lifeways and experiences, Cree poet Nia To Go There's poems illuminate, challenge, inspire and educate"-- Provided by publisher.

Identifiers: LCCN 2025016601 (print) | LCCN 2025016602 (ebook) | ISBN 9798896560388 (paperback) | ISBN 9798896560395 (hardcover) | ISBN 9798896560401 (epub)
Subjects: LCGFT: Poetry.
Classification: LCC PS3620.O2 M38 2025 (print) | LCC PS3620.O2 (ebook) |
  DDC 811/.6--dc23/eng/20250616
LC record available at https://lccn.loc.gov/2025016601
LC ebook record available at https://lccn.loc.gov/2025016602

dedicated to everyone who aspires to understand

"I think love is not a bridge at all:
I think love is a hyphen,
An umbilical cord...."
—Bayo Akomolafe

contents

preface

dear reader:

cree does not capitalize any words so i decided to use only lower-case letters and i found that without the use of capital letters my entire being began shifting away from the single perspective of the "i" to one broadened by a panoramic experience of shifting voices in our human and other than human world freely expressing geographies of the heart in unique and mysterious ways. my apologies if this is confusing.

cree and métis are still very much spoken languages with nuances and beauty that expands over time. hopefully, i am not misrepresenting these languages i heard while growing up but never learned to speak very well because my parents were told that our native languages would interfere with learning to speak "proper" english. today i transcend the hierarchical classifications and objectification of things and people embedded in the english language by writing poetry and poetic prose—a reminder of my indigenous roots that are alive and entangled in this "cosmic dance" we call life.

ki ta ta mi in, nia

introduction

matwân cî is the wonder i find in life constantly unfolding
within these existential and perennial questions:

it is so essential to ask, *"who am i?"* i know i am not separate
from rocks, trees, merging dualities, unknown trails, or eagles
hovering during ceremony.
i am beginning
to understand the "emergent echoes of my own heartbeat
unfurled and felt
everywhere in everything." (*yet i am afraid i may end up so lost
in this toxic culture.*)

other days i ask, *where am i?* this is such a pivotal question
in a society that calls itself civilized—a society
where people believe
in dead world theories
and build corporations ready
to buy a person's mind, body, and soul!

when i ask *how do i live?* i realize there is so much to learn:
the gift of egg songs from the sacred chicken,
mindfulness from the crow, and wisdom from the little wren
singing songs
familiar to my ancestors
of legs and no legs, wings and no wings
inscribed in fire, soil, air, and water.
(*yet again, i am slowly shifting and drifting like words that ache
for their own realization in a world unaware of its epochs of
distancing.*)

in grief i cry, *what are we?* is this the land of the walking dead
where my ancestors no longer dance in dreams

where we are barely surviving at the edge
of "a fruitful darkness," giving light?
(is this a death before a possible resurrection?)

i look to white buffalo calf woman for guidance,
asking *where are we going?*
she begins with a story of the sacred
return of the buffalo (*promising a re-birth*)
and she shares ancient wisdom
of the sacred pipe ceremony
reminding each of us that we are the sacred pipe.
we are the bowl—the womb, giving birth.
we are the stem—our axial center balanced within
life's cosmic energies.
like sweetgrass smoke rising, we are visible and invisible.

who am i?

matwân cî

i

i wake up puzzled by a dream where the impossible happens.

in this magical dream i am a baby sitting next to a lion.

moonlight shadows us

as we sit in silence

allowing

the infinite to be with us

and we slowly merge,

without beginnings, without endings. (*i wonder*

if dreams are the warp and weft of hesitancies and distances

designed to awaken us.)

ii

(*i gave a workshop to a group of school administrators*

from the diné schools. it didn't go well.)

to comfort myself

i drive up the mountains and stop

at a beautiful overhang of red rock.

as i step into their presence they greet me chattering

in what seems to be the diné language.

i am held

immersed in surround sound

and my response is cellular to emergent echoes

of my own heartbeat unfurled and felt everywhere in everything.

iii

while visiting the land of aotearoa (the land of the long white
cloud) my māori friends are teasing me about being a tree
hugger. they are wondering if i will pass their little "test"
that will definitively prove my status as a tree hugger.
when we arrive in the bush the next morning, they gently
blindfold me, guiding me up a steep hill and directing me
to choose one tree, which i will have to identify later.
i unknowingly bond with a totara tree, representing everything
that roots us, anchors us, and identifies us.
when i signal that i am ready,

     i am led back down the hill.

     i remove my blindfold,

and i see the totara tree
waving her long branches (*at me*)!

iv

(as we are nearing the end of a weeklong team building retreat
with outward bound, we are told we will be going on a challenging
mountain hike the next day.) i volunteer to lead the hike
for option three with an elevation of approximately
11,500 feet. fourteen of my friends sign up
and we leave early in the morning because it is going to be
a very long, long hike.
someone brilliantly suggests that the slowest hiker set the pace
by walking alongside me.

(it is pitch dark and as i lead the way up the mountain, i realize
that the narrow beam of flashlight
only confuses the terrain.
i turn it off.
suddenly i know
this trail i have never walked before.) in the rising sun
some of the guys appear to be so tall and strong
that i am intimidated *(for a few seconds)* but relieved
when i notice they are carrying the large backpacks
with our food and supplies.

about halfway up the mountain
i notice the tall guys are having trouble breathing.
after a rest and lunch break,
we continue with our slow, deliberate pace
making sure no one is left behind.
in the last stretch we form a circle, holding hands
as we ascend *(in so many ways)* this *(primal)* summit together.

literally feeling on top of the world
we are jubilant and elated and everyone is talking, laughing,
and *(hoping we are enough.)*
the moment quiets down
 as we look out upon the vista and the soaring eagles.
a friend reads the lyrical poetry of pablo neruda
and we feel as if we're on fire in the sun.

misiwê

i belong
in the unfolding hour of my minute.
the sum of my totality
conjoined
        in presence
birthed
        rooted
in my ancient past
grounded
        in the near-scape and the far-scape
                held
        in the stillness of a dark night standing within
unspoken secrets
                of sun to moon
                and moon to stars
        so delicately
        so beautifully
                holding me,
        permeable and continuous
                        i am. (*this
                        is who
                i am.*)

re-birth-ing

there is no quandary between god and self
(*if one knows*)
we are one.
we are   indistinguishable

                                paired

                                  identical

interchangeable

                        coupled.

              the very same.

we are a repetitive creative act giving birth
again, and again, and again.

awinana?

i am from brown eyes, as deep as earth's movements,
sifted and woven within dreams, smiles, sunshine, and clouds,
imagining a life filled with more
laughter, music,
         and hope.

i am the daughter of the man who wears thunder
with a promise of rain.
he carries sunshine when he laughs,
and our gardens grow. quite often, lightning and earthquakes
are the main characters in his story.
my brothers, my sisters, and i relive chapter and verse
of similar storms,
embodying days of rocks and days of wheels.

shadowed within her light,
i am the daughter of "cracklin' rosie." i miss her slow gait
across my life's path. she is moonlight waning
in the heat of the scorching sun.
gradually, like the waxing moon, her stories gain power,
and she weaves magical tales (*like spider woman*)
         telling the sun when to rise and when to set.

rose (my mom)

she stands in the middle (of the large lawn)
gazing at the small flower
gazing back.

each morning her goal is

to find strength.

to look.

to gaze.

together, they

stand in that

middle place,

directly beneath

her heart.

home

 i am sitting in a small corner of our house,
watching my mother cook fried onions for my sister's cold.
tired of this scene i jump up to run and play but stop
suddenly, watching for the huge rooster,
who wants to peck out my eyes if he gets a chance.

in the nearby slough the wrens and sparrows seem
to be squabbling. or maybe sharing news and stories.
i wish i understood their chatter.
are they telling tales of victory or tales of woe?
or a good joke that shakes the tree branches?

next door, grandma (kôkum) hums as she cooks.
grandpa (môsum) cusses loudly
at the damned cow that kicked him in the shin yesterday.

my cousins and i wander out into the woods protected
by our three-legged dog, rex.
he follows us wherever we go.

back home, kôkum feeds us warm biscuits with commodity
peanut butter and homemade jam.
for supper we will probably have fried chicken.
i am secretly hoping it's the rooster.

how like a mouse i be

the trap is waiting.
loaded with brown peanut butter,
cream cheese and other tasty morsels.
yummy!

quietly tiiippy tooooeing
she creeps,
looking right, looking left.

cautiously,
so cautiously she approaches,
eyeing and anticipating a feast.
she blinks.
moves in.
the trap snaps.

smiling she sits
nibbling
thinking. hmm.
i could make a habit of this.
so tasty.

i am quite a mouse.
yes, i am!

speaking in tongues

black as de sky
is scared (and scarred) witout starz.
he stood der.
      "can i axe you a question?"

"me? i tot you wuz talking to someone else. surry."
"whut did youz want to ask?"
      "well, is you a mixed blood?
      or a real native person?"

i answered de best i could dis day
cuz i wuz tinking of biocentrism i jest read so
i sed, "we wuz all an illusion wit aspirations
of being
      de sum of one someday soon."
      he smiled.
      "me too."
our talk wuz good. and i understood.
his question and de answer dat came to me.

kôna

i think of snow as a fourth phase of water,
not liquid,
not ice,
not vapor.
it is an uncategorical self
with texture and just the right temperature

to be in-between.

it has the pull of gravity holding its essence
in such a way that it floats down
silent and continuous.

and returns to the earth with murmurations *(of self)*
embedded in communal agreement
uncategorical

and in-between.

origins

i grew up on

the turtle mountain reservation in northern north dakota.

the winters are nearly unbearable.

the winds howl throwing snow and ice.

in the brief time between winters

mosquitoes are nasty,

     flies are more than determined,

and the land is reticent to speak.

gradually, i learn.

 i find that the land moves within me while (*seeming*)

     to remove itself from my senses.

the stillness and shadows within the moment

     reveal (rather than hide)

     the living landscape of the turtle mountains.

i feel the earth

(*not just a specific segment of land*)

     telling me who i am.

a small question

i imagine that a grasshopper
looking for its mate
eventually couples
gives birth
and ultimately returns
to the soil from which it came.

(i have a small question. . .)

when taking a backward glance
how does this beautiful being know
 its past
is firmly embedded
within the moment?

miyo

life is

      an upward trajectory of winged voices

aligned

      along curvatures of shifting clouds

      held within the constancy of blue

(*of course*)

not forgetting crawling creatures contoured to hills and valleys,

      greening with emergent seedlings waiting

to be voiced *(to be storied)*

      vibrating (*almost urgently*)

with cellular persistence having been housed

(*just)*

beneath earth's skin

until

fully purposed.

      life is. . .

      re-member-ing.

the sun gazing dance (to cam)

the medicine man asks me to tie prayer flags
onto the cosmic tree. these flags represent the colors of all
the people: red, yellow, white, and black.
i kneel in presence
within this mysterious vertical and horizontal reality wondering
who i am in this cosmic dance.
eagles hover over me the entire time and i am fundamentally
entangled within this "soulstice."

as white buffalo calf woman
i smoke the ceremonial pipe with the medicine men
and singers. i witness the movement of stillness
understanding what it means to be fully
within a seamless, transparent awakening
of worlds within worlds, where the past is simultaneously
the future and the present.

the fifth direction of the pipe ceremony resonates
with our neurological urge to wholeness.
the songs sing the singers
creating a bioenergetic record the dancers
engrave on their chests.
and they are forever oriented to the "sun" —an inflection
of ancestral wishes and dreams
ready to birth the world.

where am i?

so civilized

being civilized isn't necessarily an asset. (*it confines, imprisons,
and shrivels us beyond recognition of our species.*)

i look around and i see.
my neighbors as close-cropped as
their manicured lawns,
always weeding, always pulling the nasty dandelion
that dares to show a bright face.

"keep off the grass!" is an un-spoken rule.

when a weed crops up in the neat life,
they are there with weed-b-gon.
arresting any unwanted growth.

(occasionally, i find myself pulling weeds.)

the box

i began thinking of the box (*in a different way*) when a wise man
tells us "don't try to think outside the box but stay inside to find
its limitations, its fragility, its weakness and crack it wide open."

the box has been incognito far too long.
there is grave concern now because it has essentially infiltrated
the cultural view of the entire world.
categorical thinking, political divisiveness,
economic predation, and ecological degradation based on "dead
world theories" are some of its' influences.
houses, buildings, and other structures are built in the shape
of boxes, creating walls of isolation.
this boxed perspective is cementing our landscape with roads,
sidewalks, and parking lots to make sure we don't muddy
ourselves. this same thinking is building underground sewers
to protect us from our smelly refuse and constructing large dams
to protect us from the floodwaters of despair.
there is hope though.
more and more human advocates are figuring out ways
to flatten the box.
their conjecture is that the earth will still be round,
but it will also be flat.

passages

yes, he's twelve months old today!
little man walks slowly with tentative steps the size of his years.
he is a new page in the family album.
his mom smiles and tells stories of her baby's adventures.
fascinated when her child points and gurgles demanding
with urgency exactly what he wants. now!

(the relatives and friends sit around and smile, celebrating his
happy birthday. snippets of their conversations sound like this.)

> "i take twenty-seven different pills, and my p.a. says
> she's going to change some of my prescriptions, so i
> don't have too many side effects. i swear if roseanne
> doesn't go see the doctor soon, we'll be going to her
> funeral. the only reason i've made it to sixty-two is this
> new pill that just came out and it seems to be working
> except it's hard on my liver, the doctor says."

growing up is to know what lies ahead and to predict the illness
of each decade with single-minded accuracy:

1. diabetes in your mid-thirties,
2. sore knees and aching back in your forties.
3. congestive heart failure in your fifties.
4. a walker with a padded seat cushion in your early
   sixties.
5. a lovely room in the assisted living center in your
   mid-sixties.

6. the nursing home as the final stop in your late

    sixties.

(and the conversations continue.)

    "oh, never mind.

    pass the pork sausage and prime rib.

    i can hardly wait for the ice cream and pie!

    and there's the double-decadent chocolate cake.

    yummy, everything is so good!

    will there be enough for seconds?"

a fish story

*(a story is the shape of a life, often hidden within unprobed
depths.)*

the clouds are beginning to gather, but no problem.
i am told that fishing is especially good
        on days without the sun.
hooked and thrown back in.
i ponder how the fish tell their stories of catch and release:
        tales of a malformed eye.
        a scarred cheek.
        a broken heart.
        a hesitancy to take chances.
do they experience post-traumatic-stress-disorder?

the weather forecast predicts at least twelve inches of snow.

(i marvel about the life of
a snowflake.
the sum of its parts
condensed from
breath, oceans, lakes,
and rivers.
each flake a star-shaped
wonder
a crystal lattice,
a hexagonal beauty,
a complex, stellar
phenomenon.)

in the village, night settles in until the alarms go off.
showers are hot and steamy, dogs are out on their morning walk,
cats are yawning and stretching.

    in early morning the snowplows are awakened.

    the roads need to be cleared.

    school buses need to run on time.

    people need to get to work.

(an ordinary day up north, oblivious
    of this foot of wonder.)

are we or are we not a weed?

do you ever ponder what makes a weed a weed?
i was puzzled by this when i learned that the beautiful
morning glory flower is categorized as a weed!

according to my research any plant is a weed if it is growing
in a location where it is not wanted because it chokes
the landscape, killing all other plants.

in the news, i read so many stories where some human beings are
unwanted and seemingly out of place because they are polluting,
compromising their integrity, and generally acting (out) in
destructive ways.

they are weeds.

it seems to me meaningful adaptive, survival skills assume a
willingness to change, to transform, to stay rooted, to be integral
to the landscape instead of trying to dominate it.

this may be the secret to no longer being a weed.

unmasked

the new bank teller is daydreaming, making plans
for the "big day." her large engagement ring flashes
as she counts the money for an approved cashier's check.

suddenly, the doors bang open and there he is, masked and
wearing her fiancé's favorite blue plaid shirt. she ducks beneath
the counter (her heart racing).

"give me all the cash you have!"

she sobs, "how can you do this to me when i just started working
here. and i only found out two days ago that i'm two months
pregnant. if i give you the money, i will get fired."

"shit!" the masked bandit wipes his brow and runs out the door.

she thinks to herself, "oh, i guess i didn't tell him that i had to
get a hysterectomy when i was sixteen years old. what can i say,
it is a teensy, tiny white lie."

she smiles, "if he leaves me, i'm keeping my ring!"
"after all, 'diamonds' are a girl's best friend!"

off-center

my dust rag disrupts the galaxies of dust
covering my books and all the worlds contained on those
shelves.

       i look at the clock and remember how imprisoned
       i am by time management—the biggest lie
       of all.
       i come to full-stop as i check off another item.
the galaxies of my own dust
in free fall

until my center of gravity
settles
and continues its course.

so lost

(back in 1492 columbus lost his sense of place.
his compass told him he was where he was not. it seems that our
scholars—each in their isolated disciplines, are equally lost
although some of them are motivated to continue exploring.)

historians are noted for being quite lost, creating revisionist
tales like manifest destiny and the doctrine of discovery (*aka*
fake news and conspiracy theories) because they are having
difficulty facing history. hopefully, they will soon realize
that their "single story" is way off course.

some biologists (who study life without dissection) have chucked
the compass and are changing course. they are questioning "dead
world" theories and are learning that human beings are not
separate from nature but are nature!

english scholars are so lost because they are confined to a written
language with a syntax (of objectification) often ignoring
the hidden geographies of the human heart—silent and without
voice. (*its liminal breadth forgotten.*)

chemists are equally confined to looking at parts and frustrated
(*and sometimes lost*) on how to describe the expanse of
wholeness manifested in our universe with its awesome power of
supernovas, aurora borealis, and other heavenly phenomena.

mathematicians are theoretically computing to infinity
 and are speculating about hidden equations and possibilities.
(*i hope they don't get lost.)* what would happen if they asked
their most advanced computer, "is there a god?" and
the computer responded, "if you say so."

psychologists are lost and disappointed when their empirical
studies don't shed light on the elusive human psyche,
questioning and puzzling why human beings cannot replicate
the healthy psycho-social life of prairie dog town
(in yellowstone national park) tenured with so much curiosity
and a strong sense of place.

hopefully, they will all be joining the philosophers who are
going on a retreat to plum village to ponder
how a tree is connected to a cloud
and to listen
to the sound
of one-hand clapping.

the problem

finally, he can see clearly with his new glasses. he feels stylish
and is looking forward to catching up on his reading. yep. he
better get serious.
he tosses a couple bucks to the drunk on the street corner.
it seems there are more and more of them.
oh, well, i have reading to catch up on.
not my problem.
he sits in silence, open to the spirit, pondering redemptive acts:
giving, sacrificing, and doing "good works." i have a lot
of reading to do for my night-class. i better hit the books!
there is this indian woman in his class. she always looks so tired.
he shares his notes with her. she is grateful.
looking more closely, he notices she has bruises. oh, well.
not my problem.
the week of exams he wonders why she is a "no-show."
i should've checked to see if she needed a ride.
yeh! i passed. i am ready to apply for that promotion!
and i am going to plan for my wedding.
we need to buy a new house.
life is good.
he hears on the news that an indian woman
killed her husband.
oh, well, not my problem.
his son is born. his family celebrates. his daughter is born.
his family celebrates.
school years fly by.

he moves his son to another school because he is being bullied.

he sighs. too many blacks.

too many indian kids in gangs.

my son is now safe.

problem solved.

his children marry. he revels in his beautiful grandkids.

one day, his son asks for his advice.

why is this world so "fucked-up," dad?

why are you asking, son?

we have a good life.

we should be grateful.

we don't have problems.

weeks later,

utterly confused, he doesn't understand

why his son commits suicide.

he cries.

why . . .?

business

for years i sat on my tongue, holding back.
then, one day
          i stood up and spoke my mind!

three-piece suits, polished shoes,
and souls
don't scare me anymore.

i now know that their wing tips don't fly!

economics 101

its smile is shrewd. it sizes up its victim, calculating
eyes,
glinting.
smiling when necessary.
each tooth—a blade.

looking for a bargain?
finance options are very low interest!
with extended payments.
how about the luxury option?

it is perfect for you. go ahead.
take a leap.
time to enjoy life!

a corporation

a corporation
is a body of persons,
legally recognized
as a separate
entity
having its own liabilities.

corporations
etymologically share the same
root as the word corpse.
a corpse is defined as a dead body,
especially that of a human being. *(definitions taken from*
numerous google searches that reveal
humans without soul looking for meaning in a world digitized
to the fluctuating markets that offer little return.)

how do i live?

waiting

the snow has been too deep. i can't wait for spring.
i've been dreaming of long walks, mountains,

and traveling the curve of sky and stars. (*if given the chance.*)

they honk.
and i know.
greening will begin again.
soooooooooooon.

yes! i say yes!

the sacred chicken

i am so surprised when our hmong speaker says their sacred

animal is the chicken. (*i think i heard it correctly.*)

one rarely thinks of the sacredness of a chicken.

at least, not in grocery stores where most people haven't seen

or heard a clucking chicken.

they know wings, (even buffalo wings), thighs, breasts,

gizzards, chicken broth/soup.

people aren't aware that eggs are chicken's ultimate

sacrificial gift, holding so many promises for their future…

like the sounds of a small chick

calling its mother and learning egg songs.

or hearing a crowing rooster inviting a new day

with endless possibilities.

presence

now is…

      a sink full of dirty dishes,

      laundry, arguments

or chuckling at hafiz' warnings to avoid stepping behind a

farting camel.

back at school i am skeptical of my students,

finding it hard to believe they are present.

i reflect on how quickly they learn (from each other) the 27+

definitions of "fuck you."

      they eagerly share this news.

i ask myself why they are having difficulty

with other subject areas? it is a challenge to engage them.

but they are each an adventure,

      with plenty of mischief. suddenly our pet rabbit runs into

the hallway and i'm back in the moment.

while chasing our little rabbit, i glance up at the bulletin board

and charlie brown is smiling at me

(*and not saying blah, blah, blah*).

i smile back knowing this is high praise from him.

i just know (to evony)

of course, we all know…

unicorns are real. how do i know?

well, i just know.

> i believe in their magic.

> when i am feeling lonesome or sad,

> i ask my favorite unicorn to talk to me.

> like magic, i feel better.

i look up at the stars. my unicorn family

is watching over me. how do i know?

well, i just know.

i look up at the mountains and i see the clouds.

playing hide and seek, peeking over the top.

my unicorn friends are watching over me.

how do i know? well, i just know.

> there are so many things that i just know.

> i feel so much smarter now…

> that i have graduated from kindergarten.

> my unicorn friends were there, too.

> how do i know? well, i just know.

kâkwa

he emerges into the world soft and furry. within an hour his fur
hardens into sharp needles, making it difficult to run and play
with other animals who want to touch him when they play hide
and seek. the upside is that his "needles" do protect him from his
enemies. his approach to the world is thoughtful. a destination in
each step. he finds it difficult to communicate his thoughts.

suddenly he notices colorful wings floating by and with all his
effort he snorts a hello. the beautiful creature answers with a
wing swish. they converse about the clouds coming over the
mountains to bring rain. in her excitement at the possibility of
rain, the wings swish too closely and get caught on his needles,
making a small tear in one of her wings. she still can fly but she
has to say goodbye. each day, he glances up hoping to see her
once again. finally, he hears swishing wings and notices them
roosting in a tree, he closes his eyes and snorts as gently as he
can. they hear him and swish their hello.

eventually, he knows it's time for him to parent. it's time to
bring a porcupette into the world. his heart is open and willing.
he understands the clouds and the land upon which he stands and
walks because of the beauty of a wing swish.

kitataminân

 there are small blue flowers along the river, and it is now
just a trickle. the forecast mentions there is a strong possibility
of a drought. not enough snow they say.
we're in for a long, hot, dry summer.
we need rain!
from now on i am going to enjoy cloudy days with promises for
the zillions of tiny blue flowers.
filled with gratitude.
i imagine holding hands
while laughing and dancing to
the full-throated music of rushing waters.

on my walk today

long grass with fine and coarse strands
ripples in the wind,
moving across fields of canola,
wild purple lupine, and oxeye daisies—
a gyrating cosmos.
>   i wonder at the stuffed mailboxes holding letters,
>   postcards,
>   bills, and too much
>   junk mail.

the small wetland is teeming with life:
ducks, geese, frogs, grasshoppers,
bees, dragonflies, and slow-moving snails.

i feel the flow of the wind.
the music of leaves and the dance
of wildflowers.
>   i am filled.
>   and stilled.

my bucket list

(love yourself. this is the first item on my bucket list.
i don't think i will get past this hurdle.
sad, but true.
to move in this general direction
i have put together some thoughts that form my bucket list.)

be yourself *(even when you're tired of listening to the same old*
stuff).
take chances *(with the determined moose standing in your way).*
learn new things *(and don't forget to replace your broken*
windshield).
fall in love *(while appreciating the woodpecker outside your*
window).
practice kindness *(especially when driving with a flat tire).*
be generous *(with squirrels, tigers, liars, and thieves).*
laugh everyday *(despite those pesty ants who never forget the*
cracks in your walls).
respect others *(and don't yell at those damned wasps!)*
let go *(but fix that doorknob so you can get back home).*

enfolded in gray

i feel the damp, thick air cool and heavy.

its moisture

resting lightly on my bones.

it is truly a gray day.

the color gray is neutral, so it seems.

but it's not.

it has an agenda.

it opens very slowly

to relationships of one note speaking to other notes

making music.

and i hear.

it moves into my core, resting.

i enter the grocery store aware of the lives that are given

that i might live.

i buy my groceries,

making sure to tell the cashier.

i don't want my chicken wrapped in plastic.

i am ok.

with it being next to the vegetables, fruits, and jars of peanut

butter to be covered with my favorite strawberry jam.

i feel loved by these packages i carry home.

i am enfolded within

this gray, ordinary day.

intelligence

is the ability to apply knowledge and skills with high levels
of awareness so says the dictionary.

i didn't understand the meaning of "intelligence"
until i observed crows, and read about ravens,
cockatoos, and african gray parrots.

wow!

crows are mindful with impeccable timing as they snack on
the interstate, avoiding disaster.

and ravens remembering for generations their history.
or cockatoos and african gray parrots speaking english.

are we humans able to speak cockatoo or african gray parrot?
are we able to remember
like the raven,
or be mindful in the frenzy of life
like the esteemed crow?

doorknobs, windows, and buttonholes

do you ever wonder how to walk on a doorknob?
or to whistle through a buttonhole?
or to open and close a window (simultaneously)
and still understand it?
i sit pondering these possibilities.

the fly jigs on the doorknob just to be his arrogant little self.
and a mosquito comes along and waltzes in the keyhole.

completely unflummoxed the window still holds the sun,
and lets in the dark while i try to figure out why the doorknob
gets stuck when i
hurry through its hesitancy.

next door one of my neighbors is creating a ruckus sawing wood.
and the fly stops showing off to check out whether
the sawdust is edible. the mosquito follows the fly.

the window closes as usual. i wonder if it is transparent
with its feelings.
does it resent being controlled?
or does it bask in my servitude?

the buttonholes, meanwhile, go in search of
their partners, hoping for a good fit.

they are leery of wild designs. and the colors!
whew! this diversity is really challenging. then the poor
buttonholes end up traipsing through the jungle and meet a turtle.

in astonishment the buttonholes gape too wide
and lose their buttons,
feeling for the first time how separation is so unnatural.

manitowan

the moment flows in and out of now.
(*its trajectory*

      often interrupted.)

now is. . .

      a gift.

      a savoring

(*of*) mystery.

it's a feeling

(*quite*) incomprehensible,

knowing

i am the ocean.

well, more like a drop

(*of*) raw material.

a creation (*of*)

pure potential

yet, fully realized.

the little wren

the little wren sings true to herself. in response the volcanoes
discipline their eruptions. the nearby mountains are welcoming.
the seas are calm. the winds are gently shifting. the sun surpasses
its own trajectories, and the human (who is listening) extolls
conjoined galaxies, knowing the stars wish
to hear more.

the impeded streams forget they can't sing, and the lions don't
go grocery shopping. instead, they settle for leftovers. the deer
don't intimidate the fences but ask permission
to pass. the cars stop, no longer wanting to disadvantage
the air from its own breath. the dogs stop barking and firmly
reject continued domestication. the cats meow with approval.

the ants begin to see, forgetting their pheromone ancestry, no
longer wanting to be colonized with the queen having all
the privileges. the flies concur. the worms reveal their secrets of
regeneration. the bees are seriously considering collapsing their
hierarchical colonial systems, and the tomatoes
are receptive to being both a vegetable and a fruit.

thunder agrees to whisper when babies are sleeping.
grasshoppers teach their locust relatives how to integrate their
intergenerational trauma. the crickets and frogs harmonize. the
ducks and geese settle their squabbles.

the muskrat goes on social media to remind all the other
creatures to watch for sky woman in case she falls through the
hole in the sky.

the sneeches, with dr. seuss' permission, are going to become
nudists. as part of their ecological commitment,
the mice switch to plant-based cheeses. the flowers dismantle all
caste systems toward the untouchable weeds.
finally, the corn plant proudly reveals that in generations past
it had been a weed.

what are we?

the rosary

it's another death.
another burial.
three each week.
the people pray, shivering in the face of the cold, white,
monochromatic landscape.
        "hail mary full of grace.
        the lord is with thee.
give us this day our daily bread.
forgive us our trespasses as we forgive those who trespass
against us."
and lead us not into temptation but deliver us from heartache.
        of too little
        of too soon
        of too cold.
killing our children (and their children's children)
        who redeem us each time they smile.

tânêhki

my little guy and i read about the transformers—sentient, living
robotic beings known as autobots
created by primus to fight against unicron (the chaos-bringer)
with his evil decepticons.

my little guy runs out to play, leaving me in my corner
of the galaxy with the ghost of my young neighbor.

(only twelve years old.
he hung himself. his body limp and crumpled, unable to
transform into
semblances of himself.)

was he able to call upon primus—the god-like "lord of the light,"
asking for his help? are unicron and his decepticons responsible
for misleading this fragile being into darkness?
why can't the transformers save our small corner of the galaxy?
i cannot help but ask.
what life comes from these deaths?
what transformations?

the haunting edge of sorrow

this story begins in the nether time, spare of heart and soul.

here life is stilled, and the rivers hardly flow.

i think of the children and their parents

buried at sea, leaving ethereal dreams and visions to haunt

pyrogenous humanity in its fevered pitch to self-destruction.

my ancestral ghosts are awakened when i read

about automatic weapons targeting

innocence, brownness and blackness.

killing and killing and killing.

this cruelty is foretold in the far scape of dreams

passed on to me,

an unknown having lost my self-identity.

i notice how the birds continue fighting for placement

on the colonized trees guarding us from the precipice

of extinction coming ever closer and closer and closer

i wonder if the mighty little spider with her stronger than steel

silken threads may be too fragile as she continues spinning her

web with single-minded persistence

even though dangers are imminent in the *orange smile*

 of the human projecting his unsuppressed self-hatred.

this is so much more than a sad story

and the river does not hesitate to receive the waters

pouring from my being.

the long walk

he stands in line, heart pounding. will they cash his check?
he just needs enough to feed their eight-month-old.
the cashier looks up, eyeing his long braids, faded jeans,
 and scuffed boots.
 "your id?" the cashier growls.
"driver's license, and tribal id."
"is this all you want is 15 bucks?"
"are you the brother of that young girl who was kidnapped.
and found dead in the ditch over yonder?"
"all i can give you is 10 bucks." "low on cash."

"next!"
"hello, sir, how is your beautiful daughter?"
"sure, i have plenty of cash."
"how much did you need?"

the walking dead

homeless.
he staggers in the rain.
bent over and drunk.
his shirt torn,
        and bloody.
his sundance
        scars visible.
his lamentations unheard by the speeding motorists
        eager for a bud lite night.
he passes the empty church of st. michael's.
he shuffles.
he drags his
old blanket
from the side of the building.
he no longer hears the songs in the rain.
his memories hear only the staccato.
rat-tat-tat-tat-tat-rat-tat-tat-tat-tat-tat.
the hotchkiss
killing, killing, killing, killing more than two hundred fifty
        men, women, and children
        now frozen in the past.
he sleeps. the four directions tangled
like his long gray hair.
his ancestors silently enter his dreams.
        their ghosts (no longer) dance.

war

shrapnel in my leg poisoning

my system. my psyche forever

shattered. i stare at the sand viper waiting for it to strike.

asking myself.

      what gives it life?

here on these rivers of sand

where i am drowning.

this land moves with the wind

      cutting me to shreds.

my soul hanging by a thread.

what am i doing here?

where death is my morning coffee.

i am a soldier. i am a protector (*of peace, life,*

and liberty) but i have given up

locked in a stalemate tug of war within myself.

      i am the hegemony of my country

without liberty.

      not so sweet.

      not so sweet.

should i strike myself?

knowing i am (past death's door). too far past hope.

too far to return home.

he bookmarks his story
to the same page.
its edges worn,
		hardly attached.

i question why he stoops under the load he carries.
what burdens him?
		is his life without love?
is he imprisoned within the confines of his routines or is he
letting us know he has lost his chance?

does he not recognize himself in the hope of the young?
in the joyous bark welcoming him home? in the tenacity
of his loved ones?

		in the choking smog of humanity's failures?

i need to know. . .
his story.
i am
		the page he bookmarks.

if only...

a noted scientist and his grandfather were driving
down a country road when he noticed
a grove of tall trees with barbed wire on their upper branches.
he asks his grandfather why anyone would
climb these trees to put barbed wire on them.
that was crazy!
his grandfather answered that the trees had been fence posts
at one time.

i am telling you this story because i see
the smoke in the sky from the burning forests
and there are more fences going up.

if only
we could change this story...
if only...
we no longer needed fences.
if only...
fence posts became trees once again.

trans am

i am racing a dangerous course,
marked with plastic,
and loud exhausts.
smoking engines. revving too high.
my rpm's in the red.
ignoring all the warning signs.
not refueling.
not stopping.
          this, my grand prix.

aspirating (barely)

everyday. i know. there are so many voices. fractured.

still holding truths. not really lost. but not totally found.

we need protection from these zombies (un-souled beings)

walking around. like, like, like, like, they own the world.

    (oh, no! i forgot to breathe!

    but just for a few minutes.

    is it ok to forget sometimes?)

i am told to avoid mirrors for fear i will see a zombie.

    (i must breathe more deeply.

    oh, no!

    my cough seems to be getting worse.)

bottled

i am feeling constrained and sorry for myself.
i don't understand this longing for the sounds of waterfalls
and rapids, and the sweet gurgling music of
mountain springs!

i live in a world of so much plastic,
in different
shapes and sizes.
yes, quite colorful, even artistic, and exotic.
>   there's dasani
>   evian
>   perrier
>   fiji
>   acqua-panna
>   icelandic
>   gerolsteiner. (and the list goes on and on…)

this angst keeps me asking. who am i? what am i? where do i
come from? why am i here?

(hmm, i suppose it is quite silly, isn't it?)

the lesson

my bookshelf holds mystics like *the journey of crazy horse,*
indigenous stories like *the scalpel and the silver bear* and ancient
wisdom entitled, *the fruitful darkness.*
i glance at some of my favorite books, thinking of my upcoming
lesson on "the mechanics" of grammar.
"huh?" my students will protest.
"why are we still studying the mechanics of grammar?"
eyeing their latest piercings, tattoos, and hickeys,
i smile at them.
in the background i hear the news of another mass shooting.
so many mothers, fathers, cousins, uncles, aunts, nieces,
nephews, grandparents, and children killed for nothing.
i use this scenario as a story-starter.

i ask the students to describe how they personally relate
to the pain and sorrow of the families, while applying
the mechanics of grammar.

one of my students writes about his mother,
raped by her father (*his grandfather*). she finally escapes
at seventeen years old.

he describes her strong resolve to live.
how she fights.
how she is steadied by her husband—a sheltering presence.
he witnesses the courage of crazy horse,

the totem power of the scalpel and the silver bear,
and he understands how his father and mother
          live within a fruitful darkness, giving him light.

where is jesus?

i go home to visit, and my mom asks me to accompany her to our
mission church. i reluctantly agree.
the priest begins sunday's sermon with this opening statement.
"i am fraught with disappointment that so few
people are here today. don't you love god anymore?"

i asked mom what she thought of the sermon.
she said she forgot her hearing aids. just as well i thought.

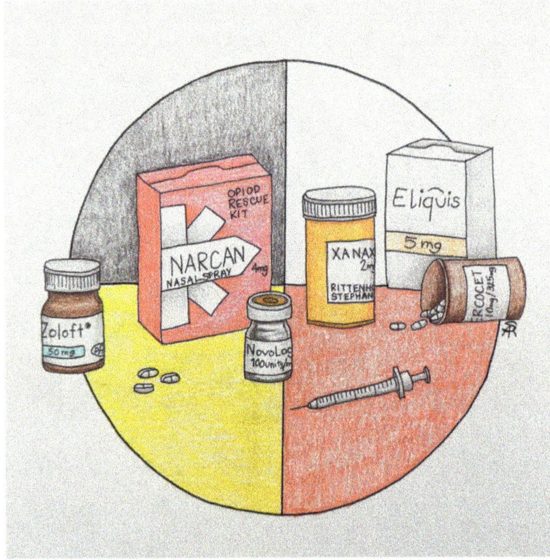

the priest did
seem quite
distraught about
something.

jesus is hardly
at church
anymore except
for christmas,
and sometimes
for the way
of the cross.

word around our rez is that he is hooked on fentanyl and had to
be rushed to the clinic
for a narcan shot again.

i see him quite often.

somedays, he teaches a version of history that makes us sad to
think that we are the victims. other days, he sounds just like
black elk when he reminds us of the "sacred hoop" and how we
are all one.

i get all emotional when i hear stuff like this.
these are truly resurrecting moments.

the cross

sad to say, the conspiracy theory of the cross has gripped
our consciousness even on the reservation. at our mission
school the entrance is armed with a large cross where jesus
and the children are victimized. they are forced to hear similar
conspiracy theories over and over and over.
this kind of verbal abuse is rampant.
i am encouraged, however, when the children yawn.

would you like to hear the real story of the cross? let's begin
with station #11 where jesus is nailed to the cross.
really? jesus escaped the pages of the bible and agreed
to the witness protection program. in fact, i saw him yesterday.
(he was incognito.) he was just hanging out
at the prerogatives restaurant.

i don't believe station #12 where jesus dies on the cross. no way!
jesus is one of the best storytellers. and storytellers never die. his
stories are rich with metaphors and one of my favorites is: "don't
put new wine in old wineskins."

(i think albert einstein essentially says the same thing:
"a problem cannot be solved with the same consciousness that
creates the problem.")

where are we going?

the sacred return of the buffalo (to janet)

occasionally, one sees something fleeting in the land, a moment when line, color, and movement intensify. something sacred is revealed, leading one to believe that there is an invisible realm glimpsed now and then when the landscape speaks ...and we triangulate mind, body, and spirit. we are attuned. the eyes, the skin, the tongue, ears, and nostrils—all are gates where our body receives the nourishment of mystery in every gesture, wing, and shadow.

for native people this timeless spiritual revelation and mystery was the metaphysical fabric of their lives. ancient animals danced in dreams—in the realm of the mysterious. the flit of a winged bird opened the skies. the thunder of hooves reckoned the flow of abundance and their absence endangered both body and spirit. they lived in eternal cyclicity. a generation of people would come and go, and come again on the earth, like the grass or the buffalo or the leaves on the trees—and the earth remained the same. they saw everything as having energy with its own unique intelligence, participating in this mysterious, creative process. tribes had different words for this universal energy shared by everyone and everything.

in the western judeo-christian tradition there are no words equivalent in meaning to the lakota—wakan, to the iroquois—orenda, or to the algonquian—manitou. what comes closest in our contemporary culture to the meaning of wakan, orenda, and manitou, is a description of the "force" given by obi-wan kenobi, the shamanic figure in the star wars films. "the force is an energy field created by all living things; it surrounds us and penetrates us; it binds the galaxy together." when one feels this "force", one begins to understand the cosmos as sacred.

the buffalo were symbolic of the sacred cosmos. their essence was incorporated into the psyche of the people so that when prairies shook with the thunderous sound of their return, it signified an ancient story made new. in honor of their life-giving sacrifice the buffalo were given thanks in ritual acts and addressed as thou (as an equal.) stories were told in their honor so that they would live on with each telling. today, i share with you the lakota story of white buffalo calf woman.

one summer so long ago that nobody knows how long, the lakota oyate, the nation, came together and camped. every day they sent out scouts to look for game, but the scouts found nothing. early one morning the chief sent two of his young men to hunt for game. they decided to climb a high hill to get a better view. at first, they could make out only a small moving speck and had to squint to see that it was a human form. as it came nearer, they realized it was a beautiful young woman. this stranger was ptesan-wi, white buffalo calf woman. her eyes shone dark and sparkling, with great power in them. she was wakan, holy. she was holding a bundle, and she sang as she walked slowly toward them. then, she said, "in this bundle is a sacred pipe, which must always be treated in a holy way. the bowl of the pipe is red stone, which represents the earth. a buffalo calf is carved in the stone facing the center and symbolizes the four-legged creatures who are your relatives. the stem is wood and represents all growing things. twelve feathers hang from where the stem fits the bowl, (from the spotted eagle). these represent all the winged brothers and sisters who live among you. when you use this pipe to pray, you will pray for and with everything. the sacred pipe binds you to all your relations and you must remember that all people who stand on this earth are sacred.

there's a commonly shared belief (in native country) that a story has potency and power because it embodies the natural cycles of metamorphosis, transformation, and regeneration. we see this in the story of white buffalo calf woman who turned into a young white buffalo as she walked away, promising she would return. she shows us how natural it is to freely shift from one form to the other, merging and mingling. there is no separation. white buffalo calf woman is telling us that the sacred pipe is a reminder of the power within each of us. we are the bowl, the womb—giving birth. we are the stem—our axial center balanced within the cosmic energies… our incense rises like sweet grass smoke…we are both visible and invisible. we are sacred and must open ourselves to our own story, waiting to be told.

acknowledgements

"ki ta ta mi in" to my cousin stephanie rittenhouse for her beautiful art, sherry lee for her encouragement, patty park for reviewing my document and providing feedback, janet lewis for acquainting me with the buffalo herds at yellowstone national park, my publisher victor r. volkman, and all my friends and relatives who are my greatest support.

nia to go there is an enrolled member of turtle mountain reservation in north dakota where she grew up. her tribal ancestry is cree. she is also closely affiliated with rocky boy reservation, her mother's home place. she has a ph.d. in literacy (as viewed from the disciplines of cognitive psychology and linguistics). her adventures as a teacher are many and varied. her most life changing experiences have come from teaching and learning about and from her indigenous culture and spiritual praxis.

stephanie rittenhouse is the child of a father who loves the outdoors and a mother of ojibwa/cree heritage. stephanie received her formal art training at north georgia college and state university in dahlonega, georgia where she graduated with a bachelor of fine arts. she gains inspiration from her frequent travels throughout the united states. her goal as an artist is to inspire others to cultivate their talents and develop a deep sense of connection to nature.

references:

- https://itwewina.altlab.app/ plains cree dictionary
- https://www.bayoakomolafe.net/
- joan halifax and thich nhat hanh, *the fruitful darkness.* new york: grove press, 2004.
- joseph m. marshall iii, *the journey of crazy horse,* new york: penguin books, 2005.
- lori alvord and elizabeth cohen van pelt, *the scalpel and the silver bea*r. new york: bantam books, 2000.

appendix: discussion questions for <u>matwân cî</u>

part i: who am i?

1. in several of her poems the author describes her extraordinary experiences where she feels a profound connection to nature. describe your unusual experiences and how you felt.

2. what are your thoughts when the author says: *"we are a repetitive creative act giving birth again, and again, and again"* in the poem **"re-birth-ing?"**

3. describe your *"days of rocks and days of wheels."*

4. have you ever had adventures like the mouse in **"how like a mouse i be?"**

5. why were you surprised by the last line in **home** when the author secretly wishes they will be eating the rooster for supper?

6. how do you relate to the awakening experience of the author in the **"sun gazing dance**?"

7. describe how the author sees herself based on her life experiences when she asks: *who am i?*

part ii: **where am i?**

1. the author cuts to the chase in this section describing western culture as not so civilized. what are your reactions to this perspective?

2. in **"the box"** the earth is described as still round but also flat. your reactions?

3. do you relate to life's **"passages?"**

4. why are we too busy to appreciate "**snow**" as a *"foot of wonder?"*

5. what is the author implying when she says that humans are like weeds?

6. explain "the sound of one hand clapping?"

7. what is the problem in the poem, "**the problem?**"

8. do you agree or disagree with the author in her critique of the western culture reflected in this set?

part iii: **how should i live?**

1. in "**the sacred chicken**" the author makes a subtle reference to how the western culture packages and ignores the lives that are given so that human beings may live. what are your reactions to this very different worldview?

2. in "**i just know. . .**" the little kindergartener just knows things. have you ever felt the same way?

3. what wisdom does the little porcupine in "**kâkwa**" share with us?

4. what is your "bucket list?"

5. describe your *"gray, ordinary days."* are they the same or different than the sentiments of the author?

6. describe your experiences of "intelligence?" are they similar to the author's experiences?

7. how is the poem "**doorknobs, windows and buttonholes**" both playful and very serious?

8. what does "**the little wren**" have to teach us?

part iv: **what are we?**

1. what does the author mean by the *"white monochromatic landscape?"* what does it feel like?
2. what is the author criticizing in so many of the poems in this section?
3. what is the spider metaphor in **the haunting edge of sorrow?**
4. what does the author mean by this line: *"their ghosts no longer dance"* in the poem **walking dead?**
5. what is the soldier battling within himself in **"war?"**
6. what is the significance of the title **"story our?"**
7. why is the author not being "silly" at all in **"bottled?"**
8. how do you relate to the author's messages in **"wher*e* is jesus"** and **"the cross***?***"**

part v: **where are we going?**

1. describe the overall metaphor of **"the sacred return of the buffalo?"**
2. how do you think the sacred pipe symbolizes the power within each of us?

overall questions:

1. do you agree or disagree with the need to "shift consciousness?" please elaborate.
2. what is the story of "separation" implied throughout the book?
3. what is white buffalo calf woman teaching us?

www.ingramcontent.com/pod-product-compliance
Lightning Source LLC
Chambersburg PA
CBHW050759160726
48004CB00002B/623